I0469851

# Thank You

Thankyou to my wife for her never ending and undying support. You are my love. Thankyou to my son who is due to come into this world less than a month from this writing. You are my inspiration. Thankyou to my Lord for the opportunities given to me to live my dreams. You are my salvation. Thankyou to anyone who purchases this book. You are my hope.
God bless!

May the Lord guide your art the way he guided mine.

# Basics

- Why the pen?

- Types of pens

- Hand Positions

# Why The Pen?

With the vast options an artist has in tools, why choose the pen?

1. Humble: With the pen there are no fancy gimicks, no brand is better than another, and style and applications are limitless.

2. Inexpensive: Pens are arguably the least expensive art tool and are largely available to anyone.

3. Precise: The precision of the pen is unmatched as a drawing tool. The smallest details can be perfected with the pen.

4. Helps you become a better artist: The pen is permanent. This forces you (the artist) to be more careful with your art and helps you build the ability to fix or hide your mistakes.

5. IT IS MIGHTIER THAN THE SWORD!

# Types of Pens

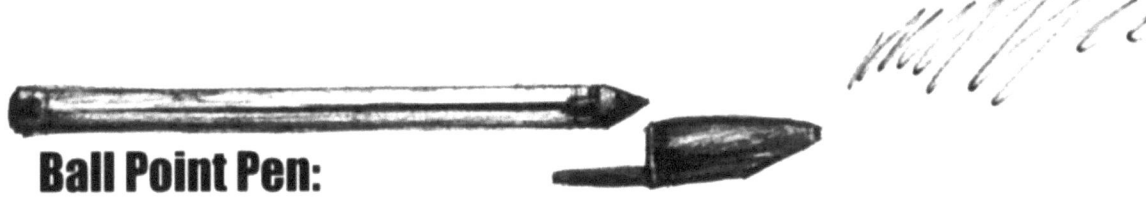

### Ball Point Pen:

The ball point pen will be the main focus of this book. With the ball point shades and details can be perfected with no limitation.

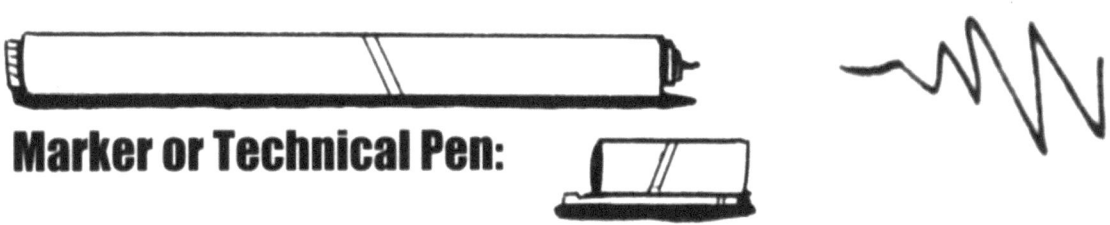

### Marker or Technical Pen:

Marker or technical pens are often used for inking. These pens are exceptional for straight clean lines.

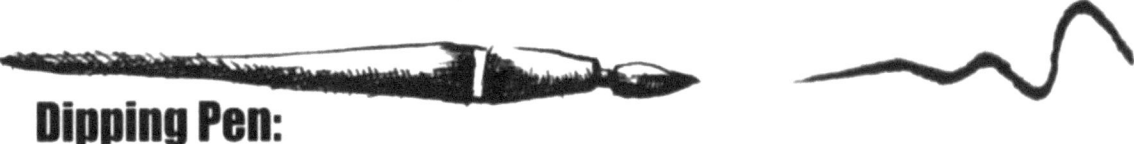

### Dipping Pen:

Dipping pens are great for the manga style of art work because of the varied line weight that can be achieved with the application of pressure.

# Hand Position

How an artist holds their pen is very important. Hand position is determined by the effect the artist wants to accomplish.

When applying fine detail, cleaning lines, or applying dark tones, hold the pen closer to the tip like in example A. This allows for sharpened control.

When building smooth gradients hold the pen closer to the end like in example B. This allows for minimal pressure, letting light amounts of ink out to be built into gradients.

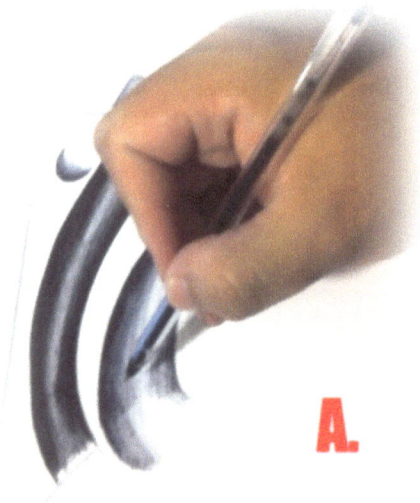

**A.**

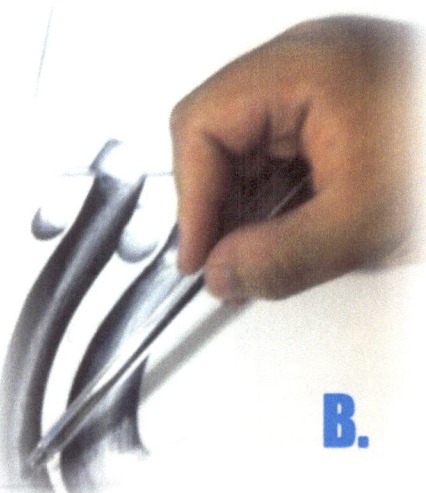

**B.**

# Gradient

- What is a Gradation?

- Dagger Stroke

- Building a Gradation Step by Step

- Example

# Gradient

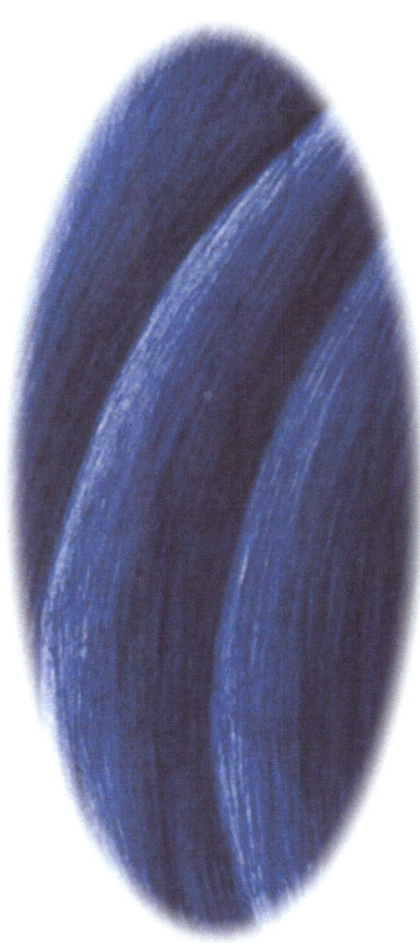

## WHAT IS A GRADATION?

A gradation is a transition you (the artist) makes with the chosen medium. This transition can be From one color to another, a shift in hue, or a shift in value. Because this book has a strict focus in the medium of pen, we will focus on the transition from dark to light. Gradation can be used with pen to create depth, shine, and highlights.

# Gradient

## Dagger stroke

### WHAT IS THE DAGGER STROKE?

To the left you will see an enlarged pen stroke. What makes this stroke different from any other line drawn with a pen? This stroke has a taper and a slight gradation. The taper and gradation of this stroke can be achieved by applying less pressure as the stroke progresses. The dagger stroke gets its name from a technique used in airbrushing to achieve a similar dagger like shape.

As shown below the dagger stroke can be repeated in a layered manner to achieve gradation from dark to light.

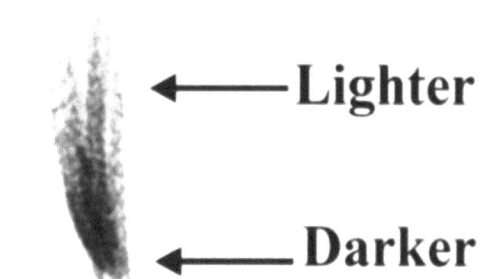

← Lighter

← Darker

# Gradient

## Dagger stroke

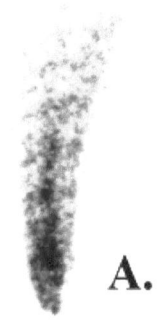

**A.**

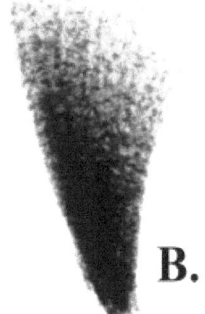

**B.**

### BUILDING GRADATION

Gradients are built not drawn. It requires great patience to build an attractive gradation line by line. Note that your gradation will not look perfect while you are building it. It is important that you do not get discouraged because all it takes is some hard work. Example A. is a gradient in progress. Example B. is a completed gradation.

### BUILDING GRADIENT SHAPES WITH THE DAGGER STROKE.

Shapes can be built with the dagger stroke by using different curves, lengths, and directions when drawing the strokes.

# Gradient

## Building a gradient

### Step:1

Lightly sketch in the shape your gradient will follow. Be sure not to go too dark. This is only a guide to make your drawing easier on you.

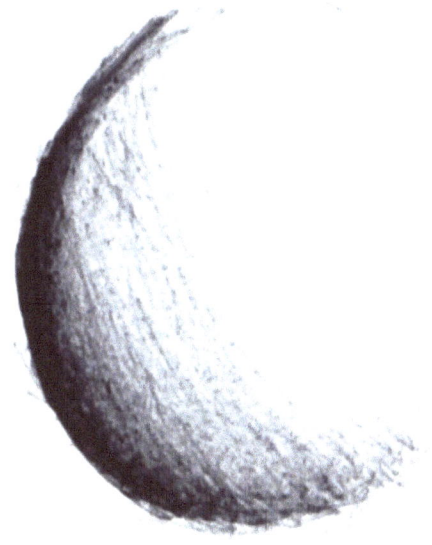

### Step:2

Lay down a basic shade applying more pressure and spending more time in the areas that will be darkest.

# Gradient

## Building a gradient

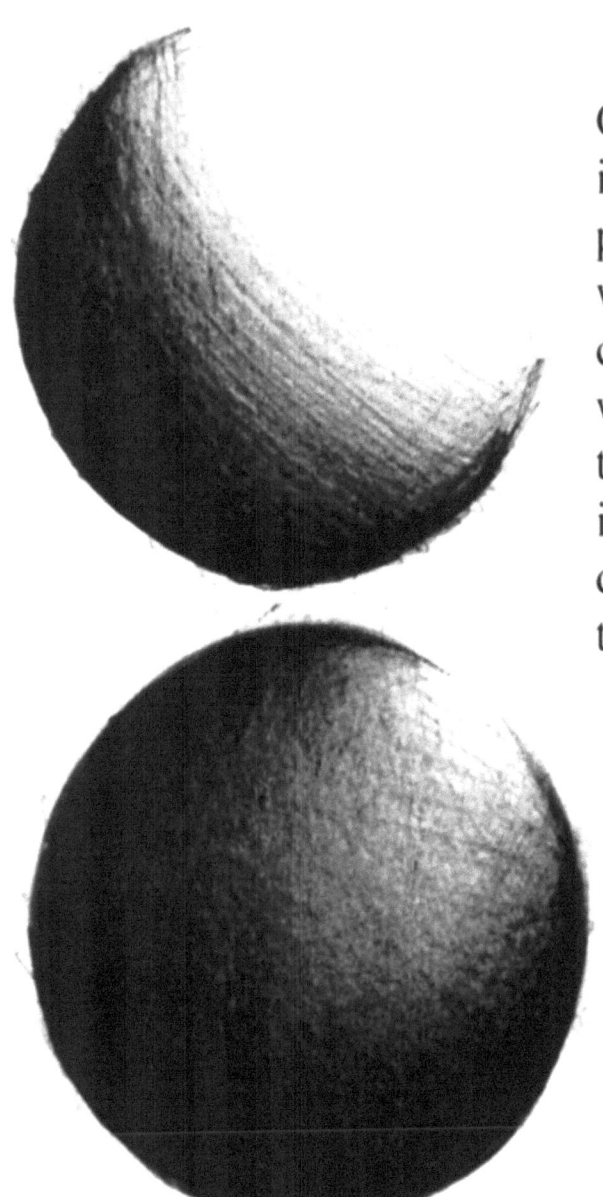

### Step: 3

Continue pushing your dark into your light while also pushing your light into the white of the page. Be conscious to maintain a workable gradient. If a streak that is a few shades too dark is drawn in your lighter area darken the entire gradation to compensate.

### Step: 4

At this point you will clean your edges applying firm pressure and pass over your entire gradation very softly, letting the least amount of ink out to blend the gradient together.

# Gradient

## Example

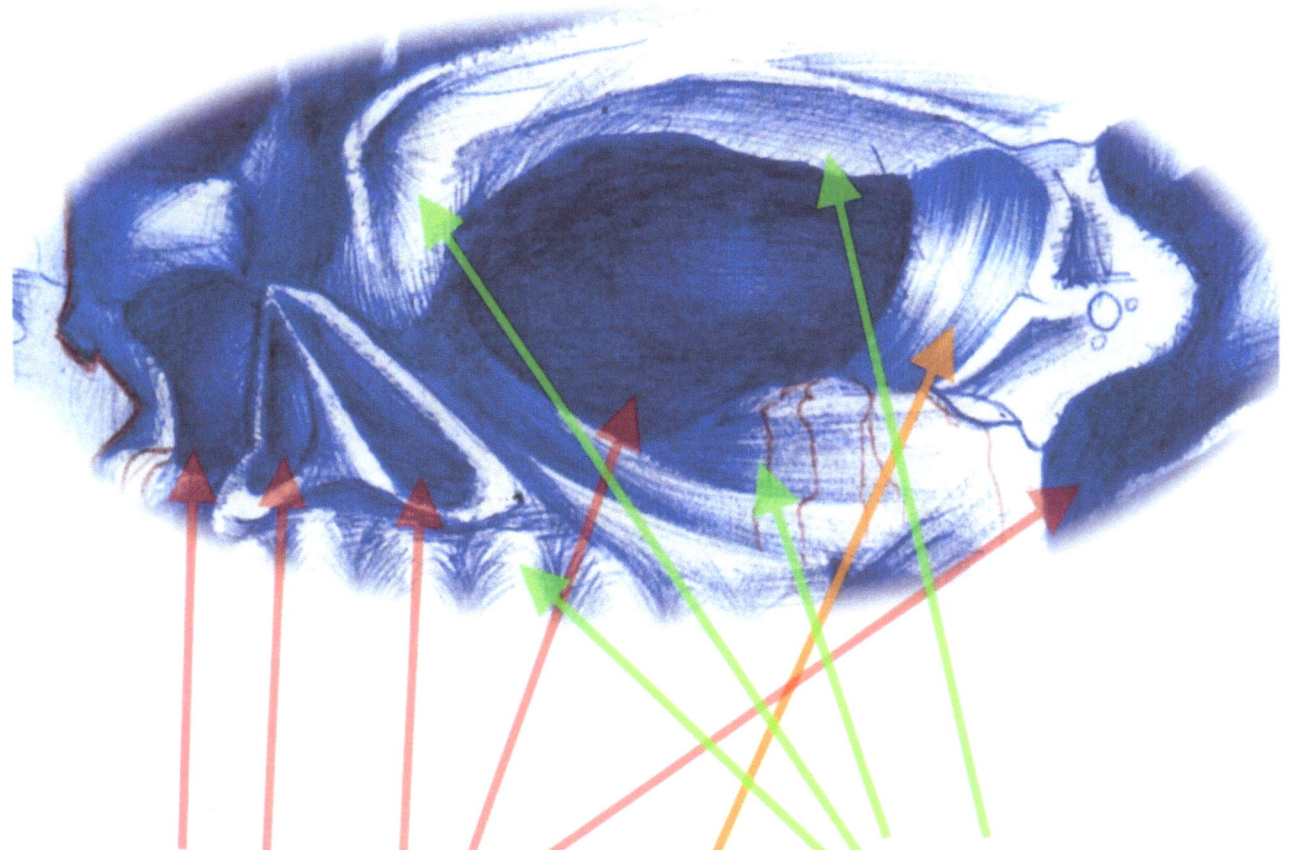

These dark areas were accomplished with the gradient bulding technique.

These areas were drawn using the dagger stroke technique.

This shine was achieved using the dagger stroke technique.

# Depth

- What is Depth?

- Light Sources

- Layers

- Example

# Depth

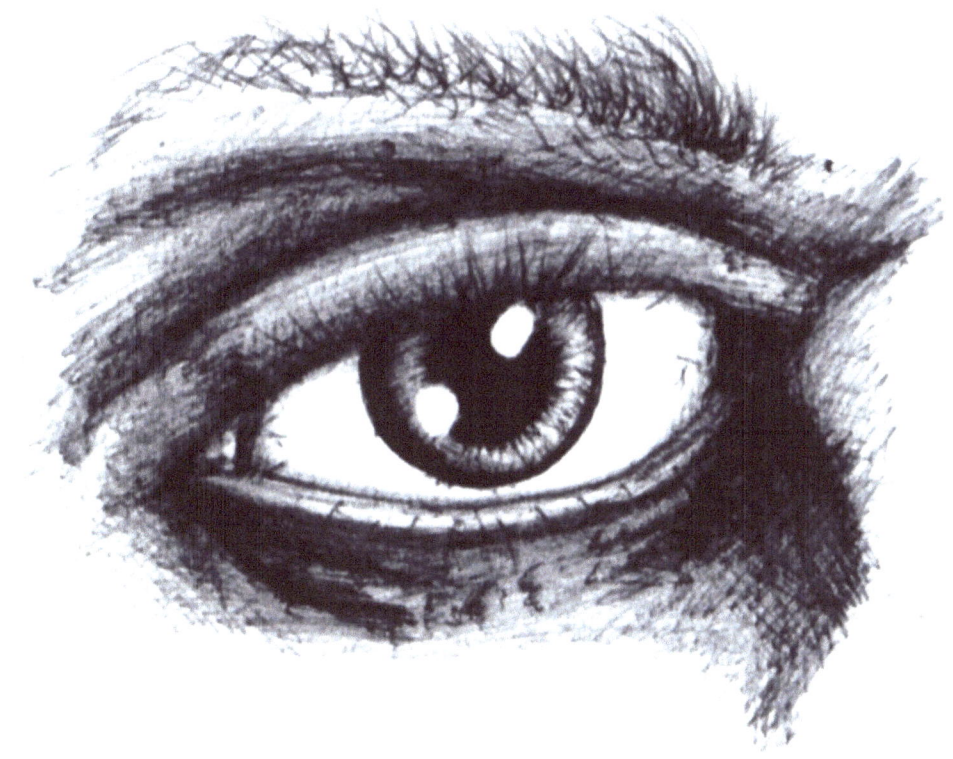

## WHAT IS DEPTH?

When it comes to art, depth is essential. Depth is what makes a flat page, paper, or canvas come to life. The illusion of depth is achieved by using gradation, layers, and light sources. In this section we will take a detailed look at how to manipulate the pen and ink to make art that pops.

# Depth

## Light Sources

Light areas with less ink require more carefully crafted gradients. These areas should be drawn with minimal pressure and lightly built to the desired darkness.

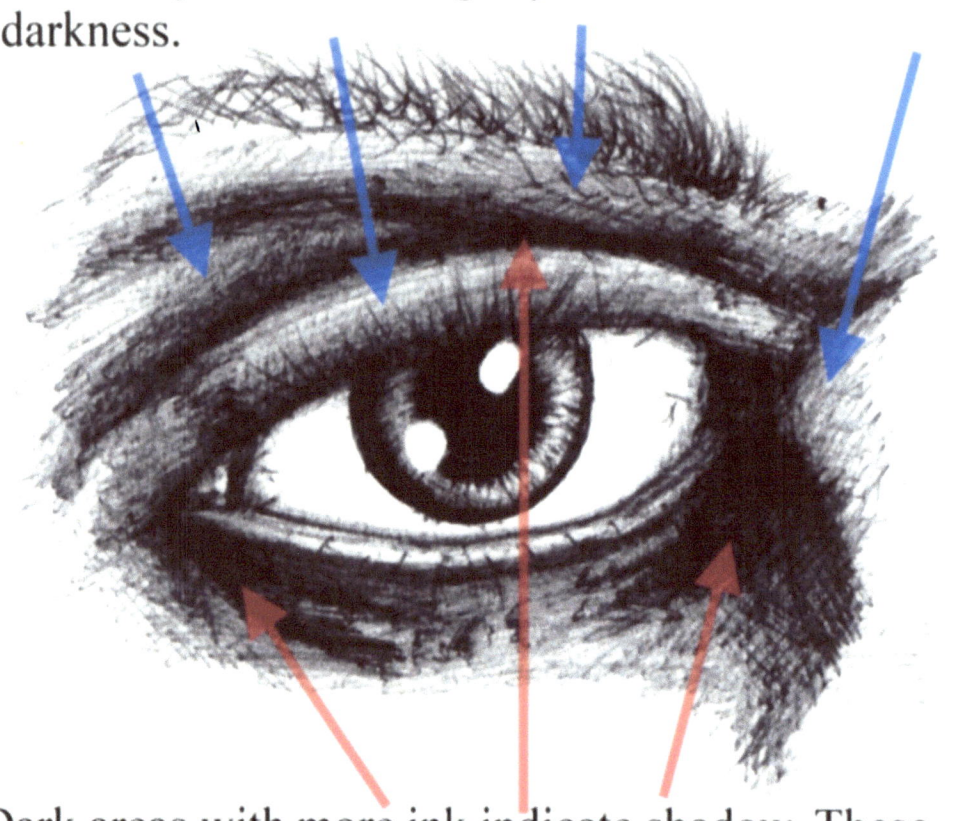

Dark areas with more ink indicate shadow. These shadows help give a 3D like effect to your artwork. Shadows typically push lighter areas to the forefront. This means that darker areas tend to sink in to the person viewing the art.

# Depth

## Light Sources

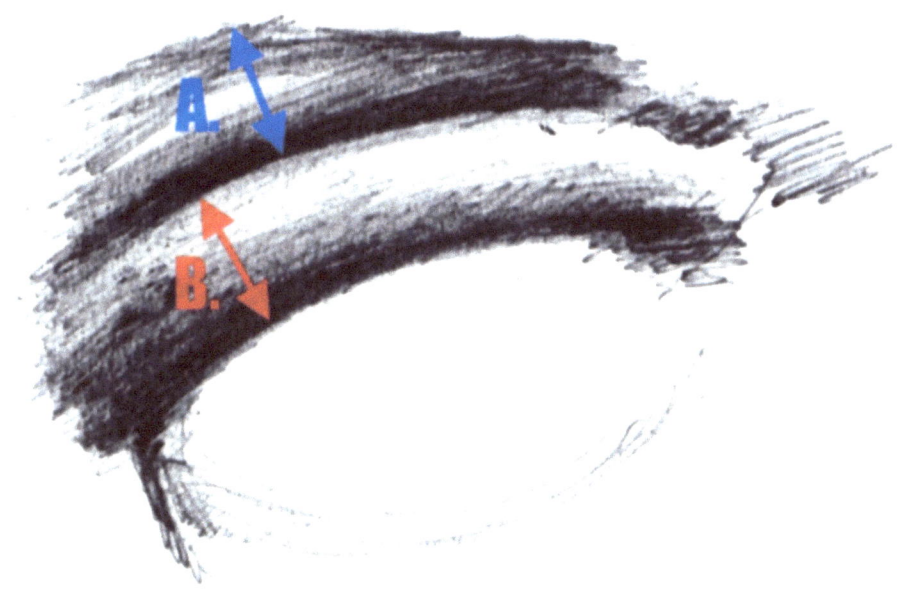

Take note that the dark portion of segment **A.** adds
to the fullness and 3D effect of segment **B.**
Shadows casted from the light source often enhance
the illusion of depth on the entire piece.

# Depth

## Light Sources

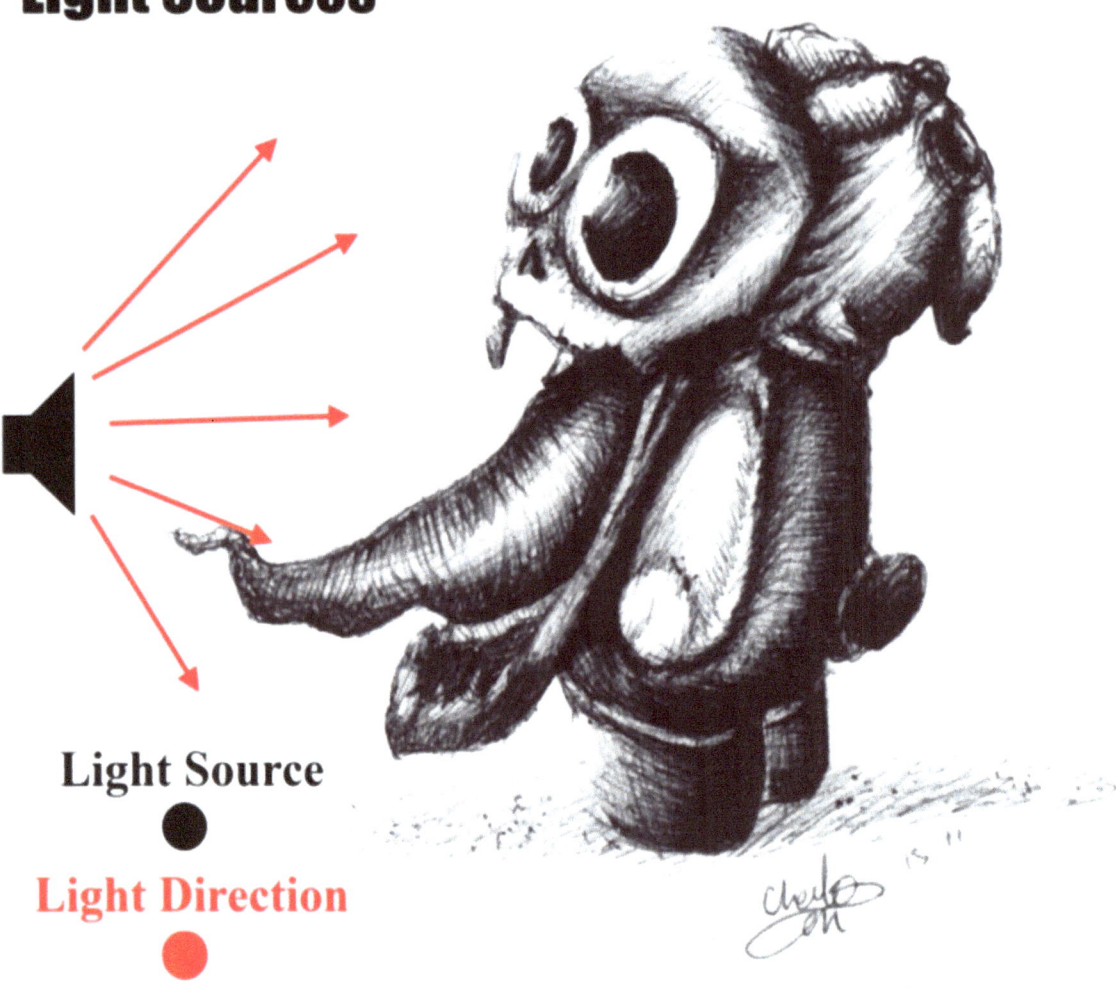

**Light Source**
●

**Light Direction**
●

The light source determines where your shadows lay. Shadows are often placed under and behind sections of the drawing that block or obstruct the light from lower sections.

# Depth

## Light Sources

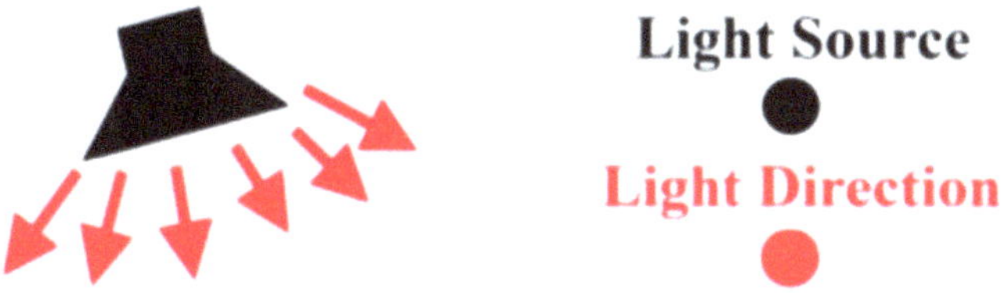

**Light Source** ●

**Light Direction** ●

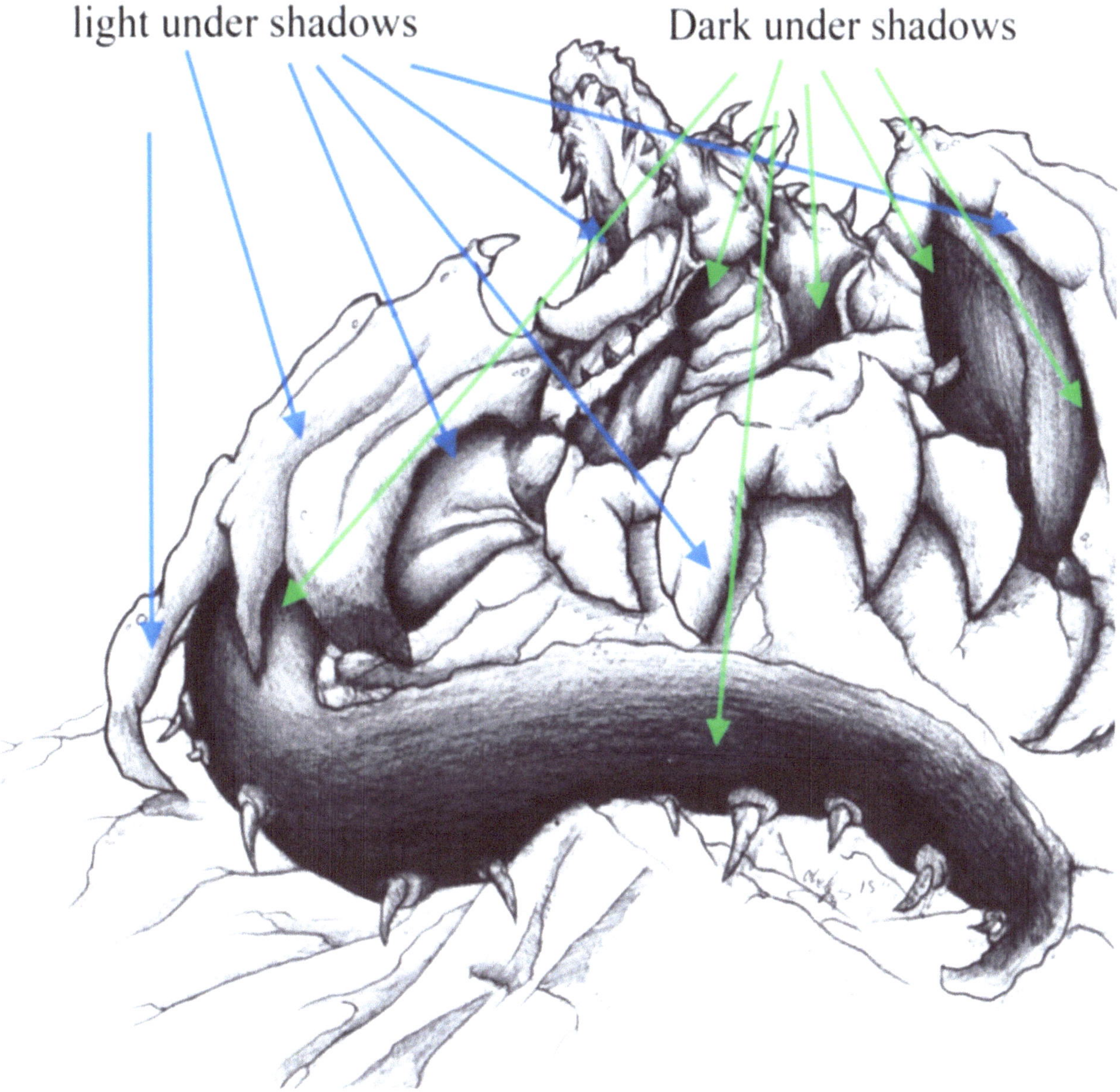

light under shadows

Dark under shadows

# Depth

## Light Sources

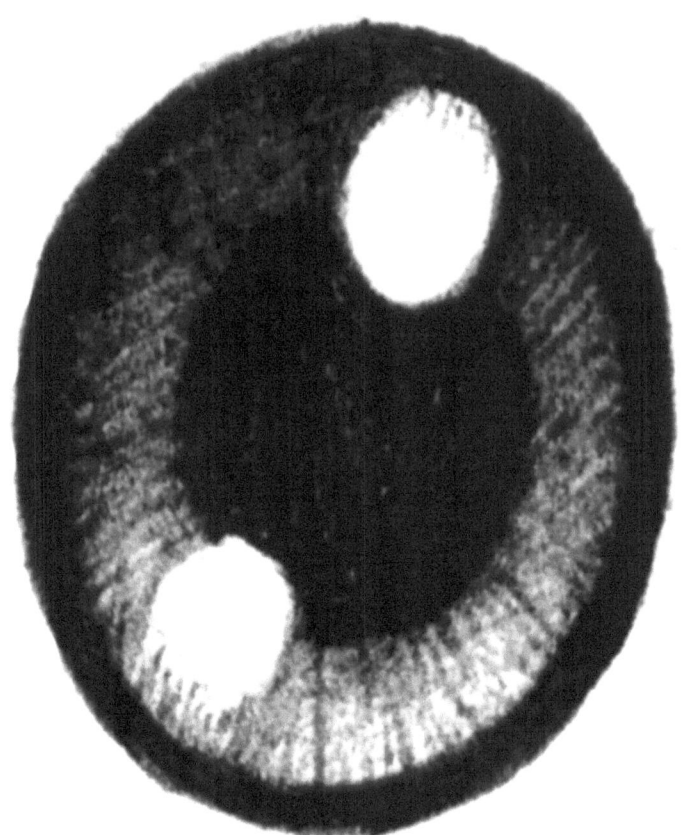

## HIGHLIGHTS

Highlights add to the contrast of an art piece. This contrast helps sell the illusion of layers. Layers are the most basic form of depth.

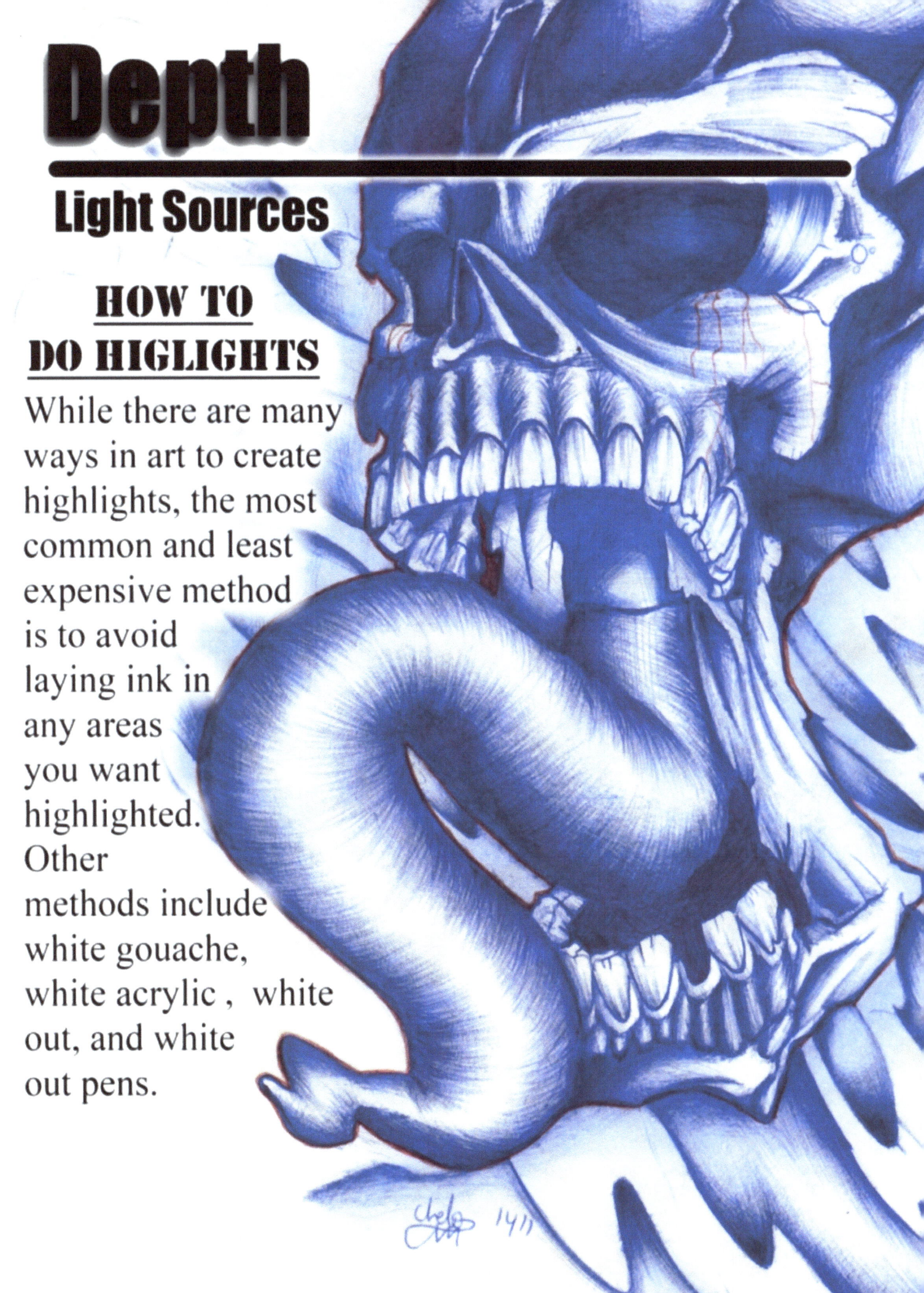

# Depth

## Light Sources

### HOW TO DO HIGLIGHTS

While there are many ways in art to create highlights, the most common and least expensive method is to avoid laying ink in any areas you want highlighted. Other methods include white gouache, white acrylic , white out, and white out pens.

# Depth

## Layers

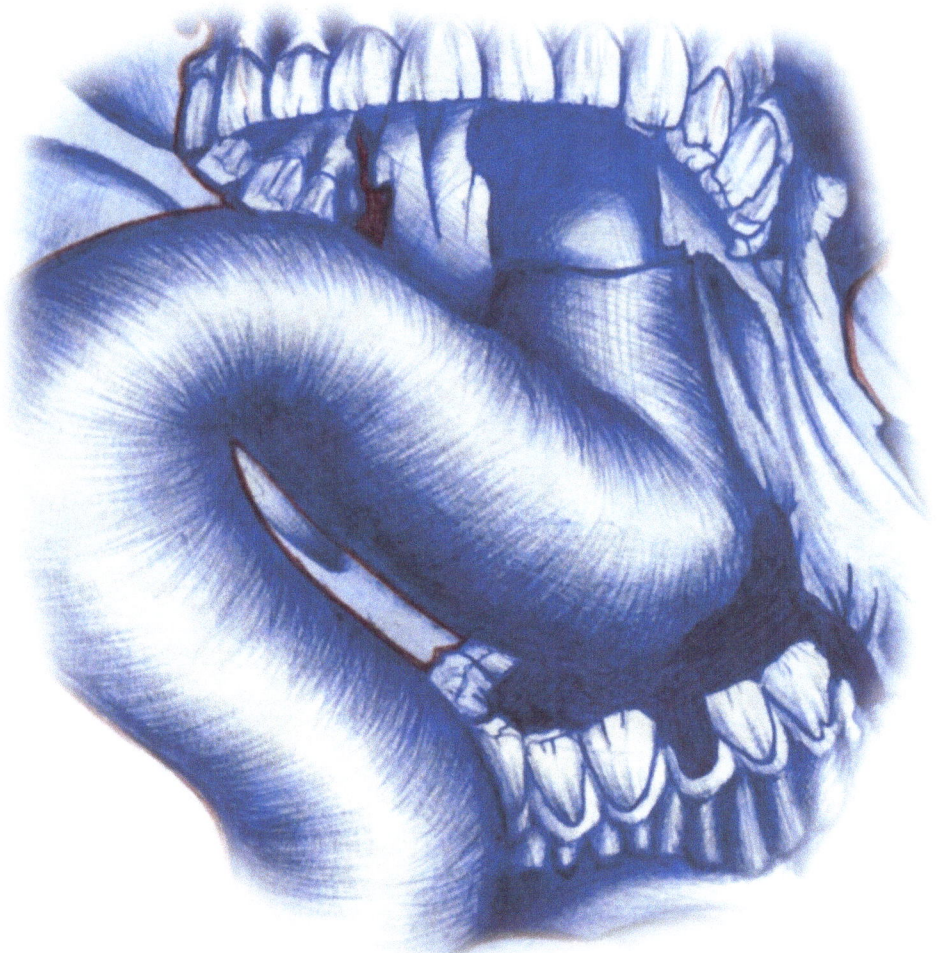

## WHAT ARE LAYERS?

Layers are a series of overlapping segments in your drawing that help push back or bring forward areas of the artwork.

# Depth

## Layers

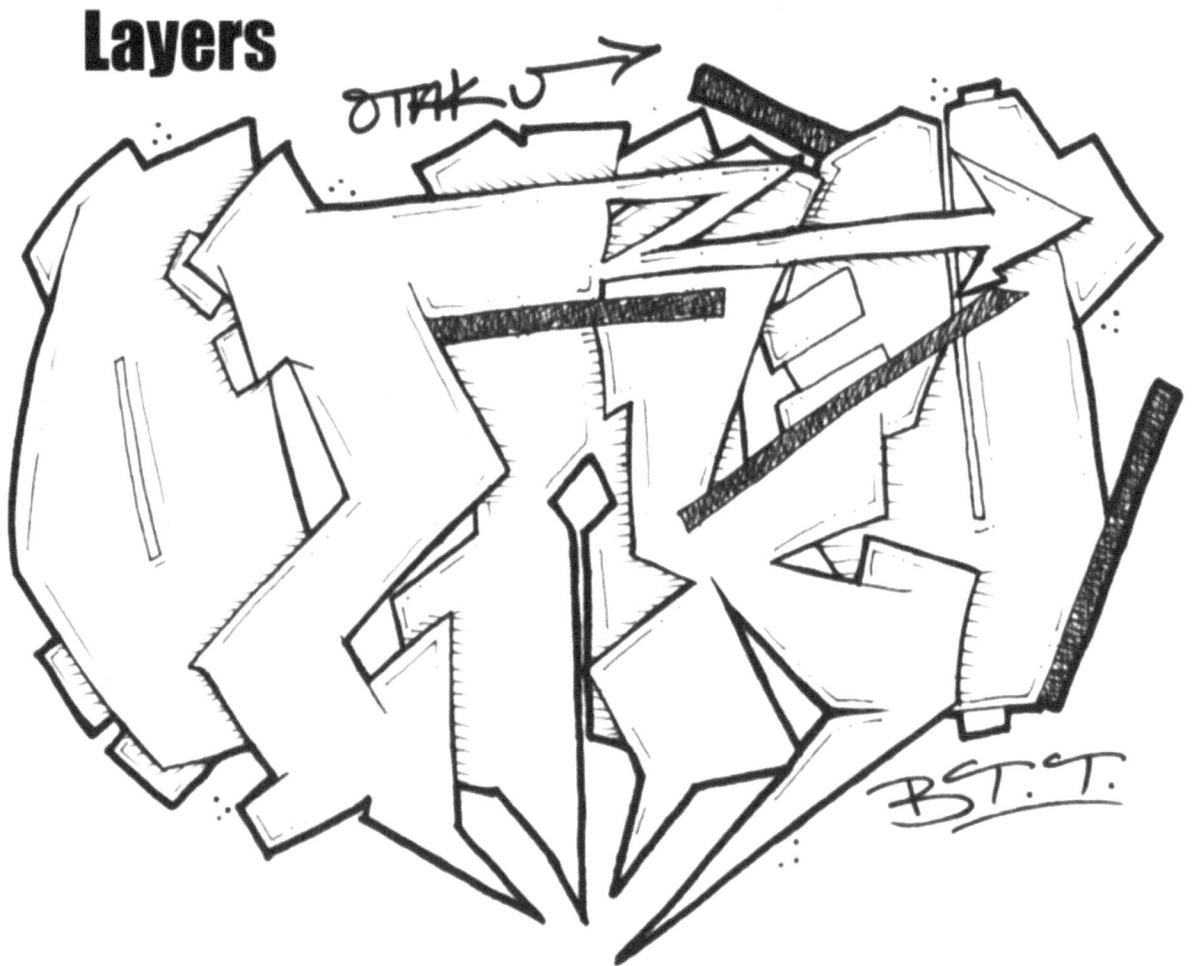

Permanent marker pens are fairly dificult to establish layers with. In this graffiti style lettering we have my street art alias OTAKU. notice that the T and the K seem to overlap the O, A, and U. This was accomplished by drawing or "tucking" the background letters behind the foreground letters, using various line weights, and using a series of whispy parallel lines to indicate drop shadow.

# Depth

## Example

This rose bud incorporates various techniques to create the illusion of depth.

Light source is used here to create highlights. These highlights round the rose bud out creating the illusion of three dimensional space.

Layers and undershadow are used here to create levels within the work. Elements are stacked onto each other to push certain segments further back.

# Composition

- What is Composition?

- Step by Step Procedure

- Example

# Composition

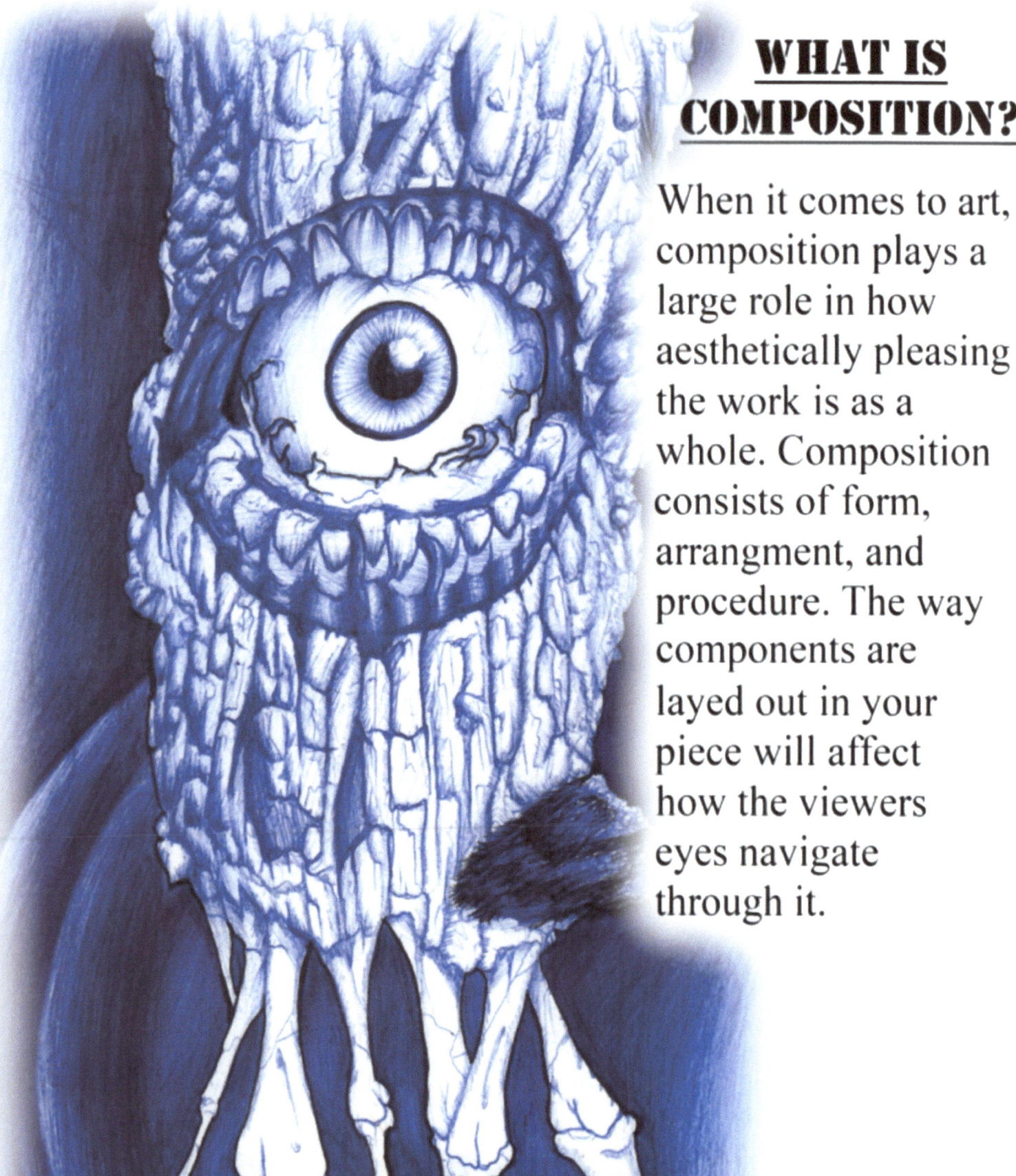

## WHAT IS COMPOSITION?

When it comes to art, composition plays a large role in how aesthetically pleasing the work is as a whole. Composition consists of form, arrangment, and procedure. The way components are layed out in your piece will affect how the viewers eyes navigate through it.

# Composition

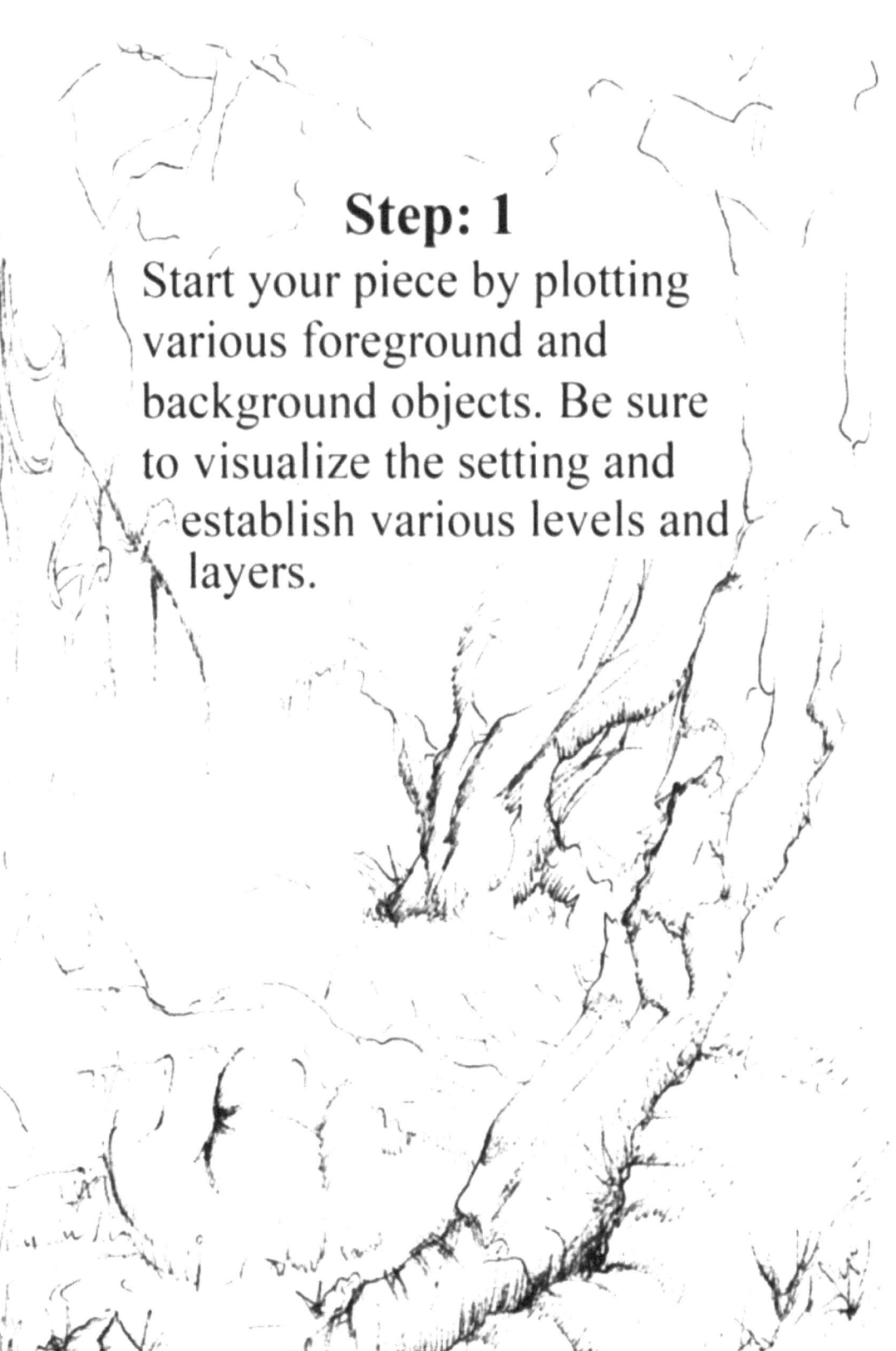

## Step: 1

Start your piece by plotting various foreground and background objects. Be sure to visualize the setting and establish various levels and layers.

# Composition

## Step: 2

Place under shadows to begin forming the shapes that comprise your piece. Don't worry too much about smooth gradients at this point note that careful attention is being payed to light source.

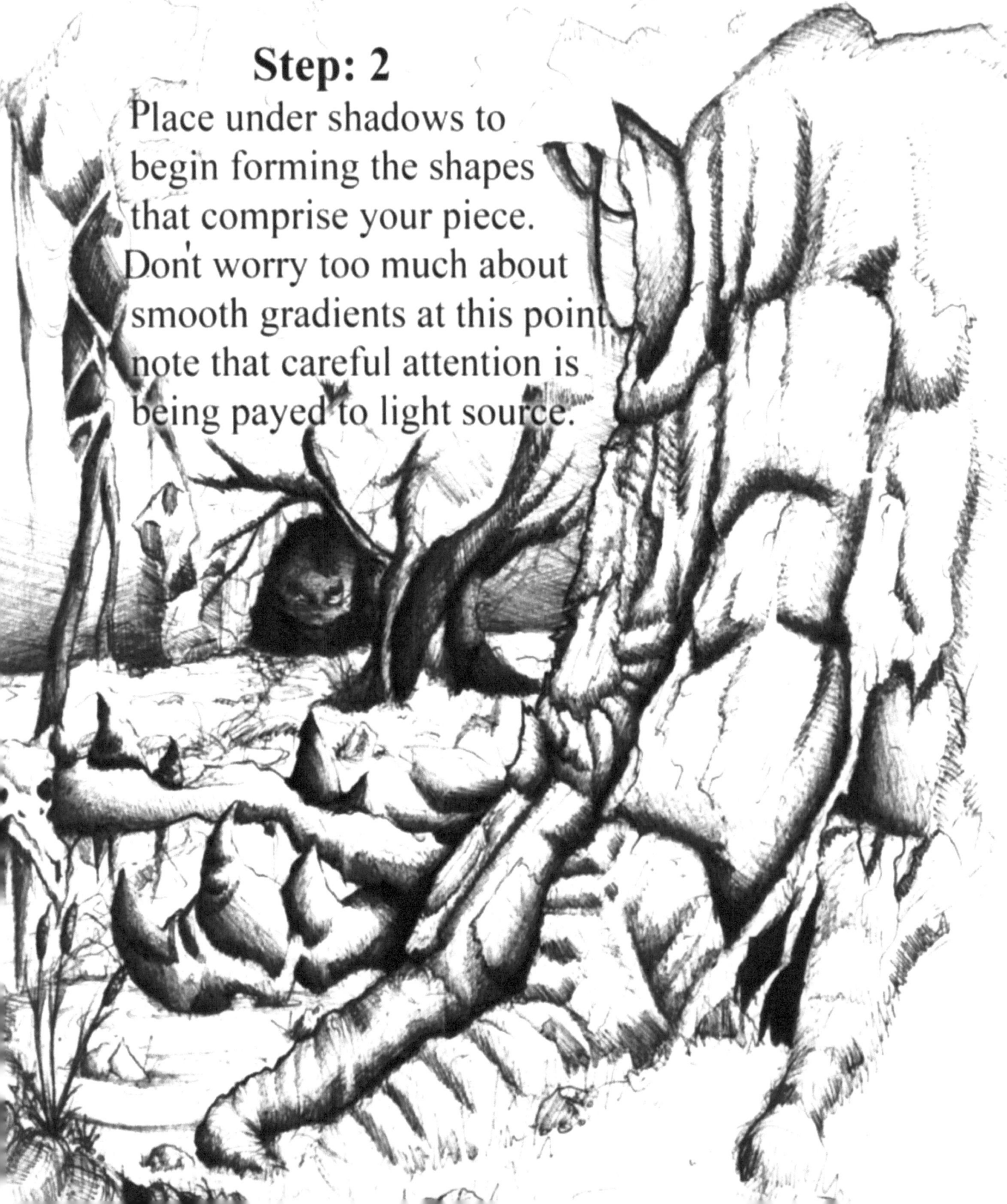

# Composition

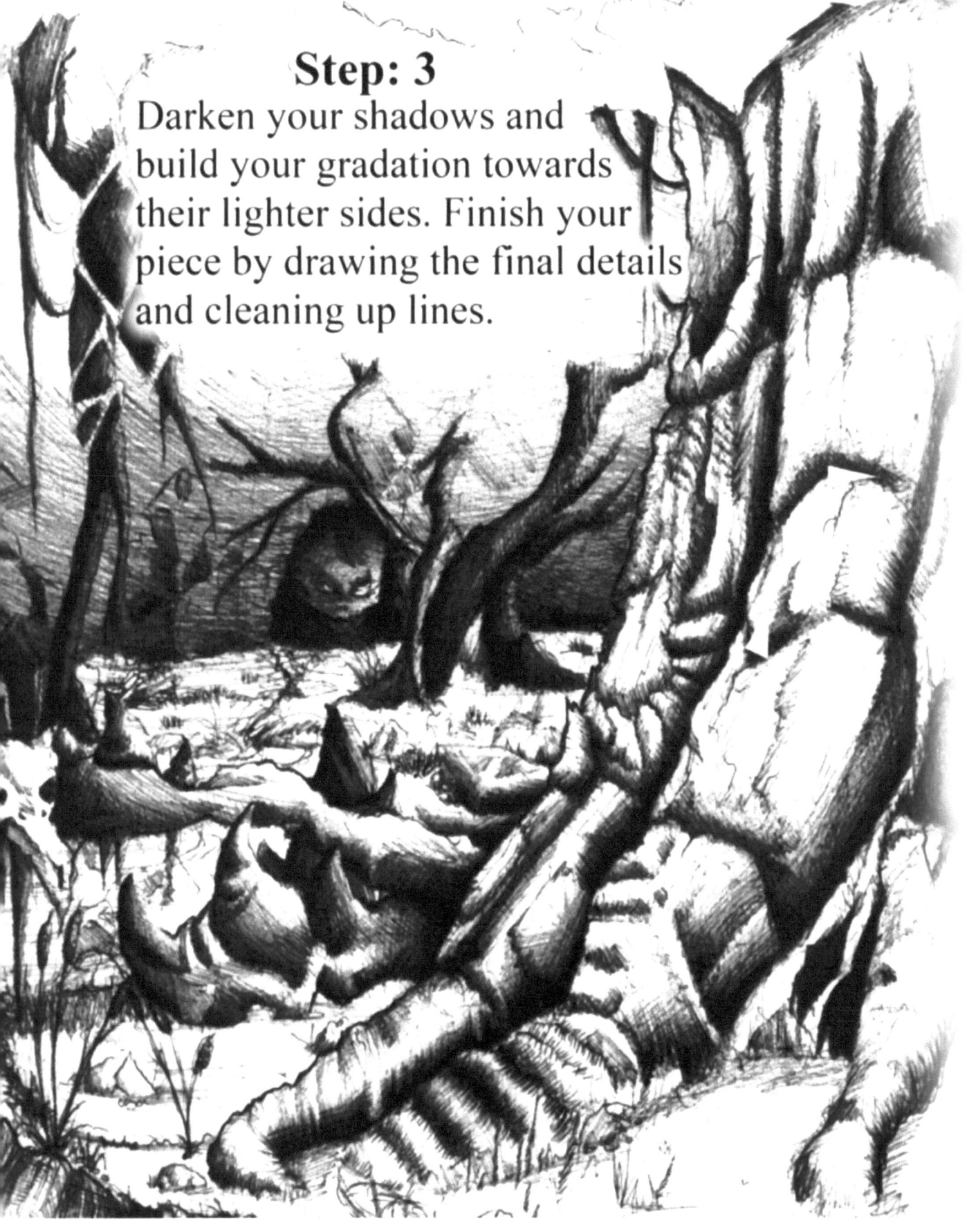

**Step: 3**
Darken your shadows and build your gradation towards their lighter sides. Finish your piece by drawing the final details and cleaning up lines.

# Composition

## Example

Consider mixing various textures and elements to achieve a fuller, more complete, and engaging piece. Forming elements around each other gives the work a dynamic and natural design. Notice how the use of drop shadow and layers brings the composition to life.

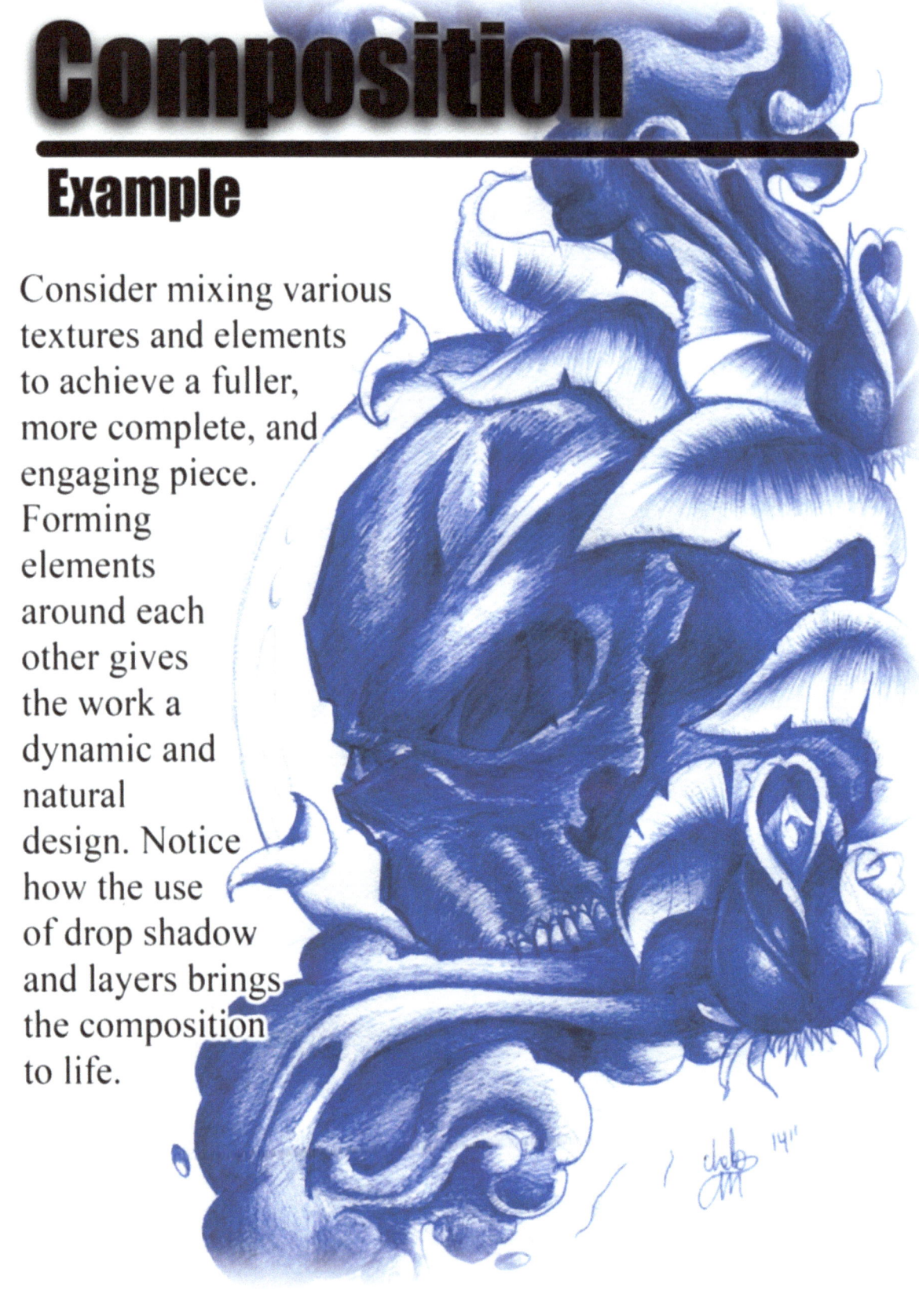

# Tips

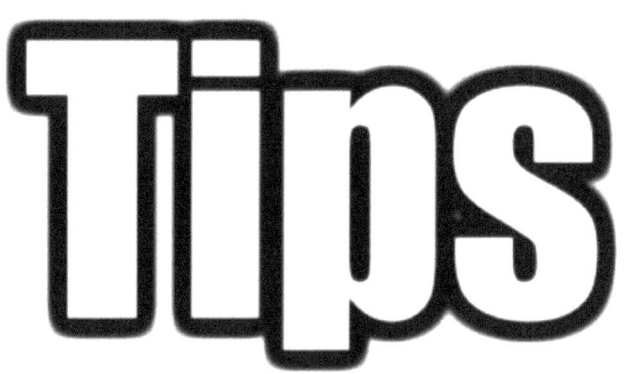

This section will include tips that will help you along your journey towards mastering the pen as an art tool.

1. Keep a piece of scrap paper between your palm and the project to prevent  smudging.

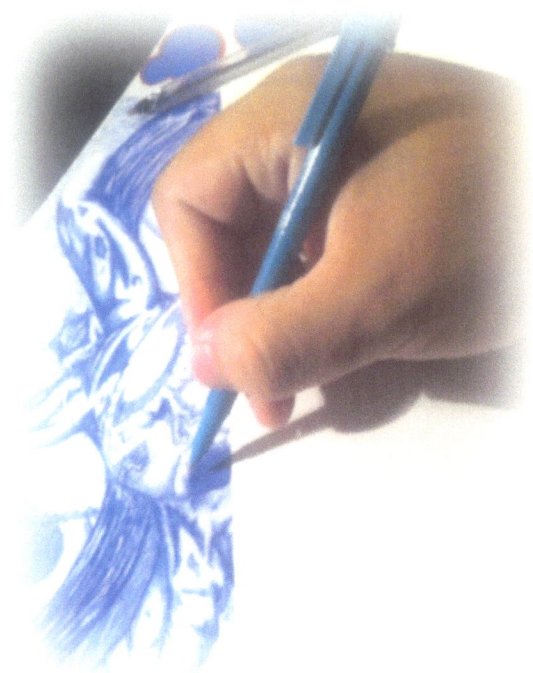

2. Wait a while before scanning your piece to ensure the ink is dry.

# 3. KEEP PENS CAPPED WHEN NOT IN USE!

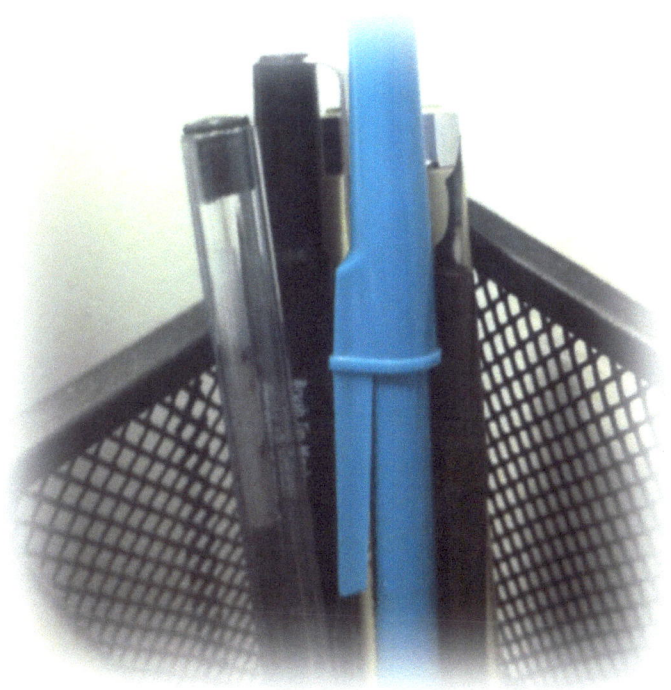

4. Keep a portfolio of your pen art pieces to track improvement.

5. Practice! Practice! Practice!

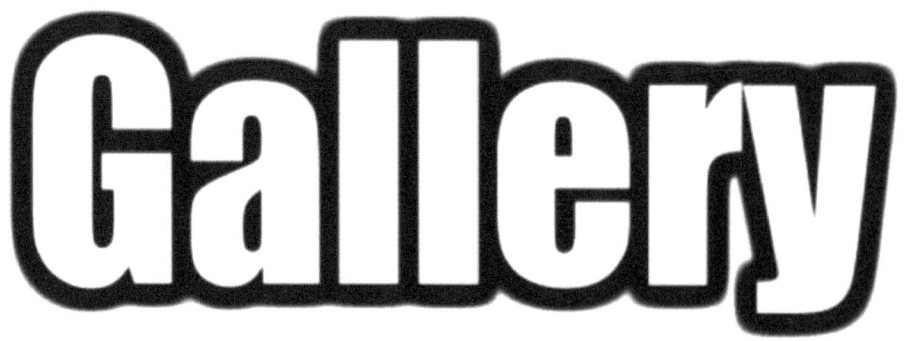

# Gallery

In this section you can view all of the pieces I used in the book. Study hard and enjoy!

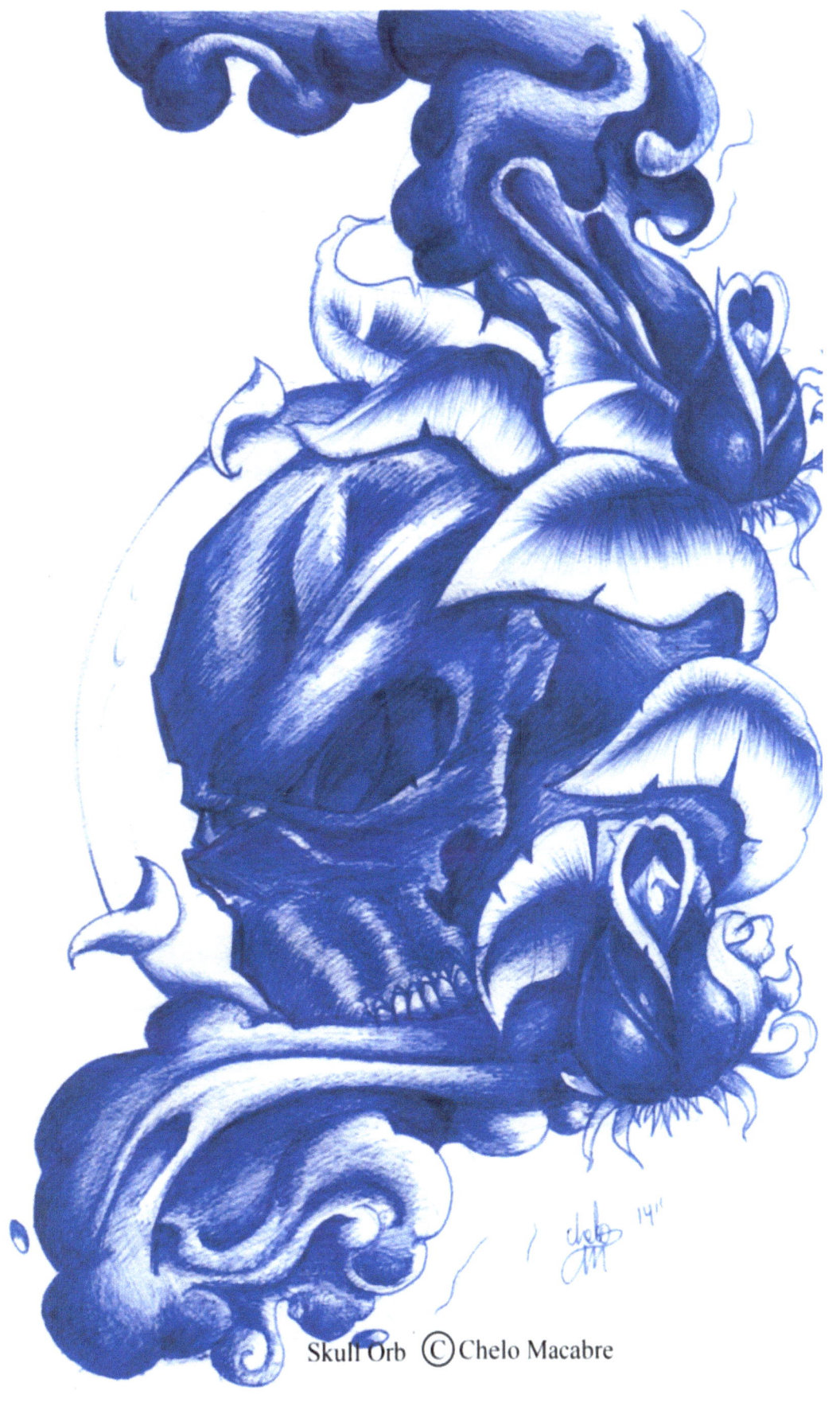

Skull Orb ©Chelo Macabre

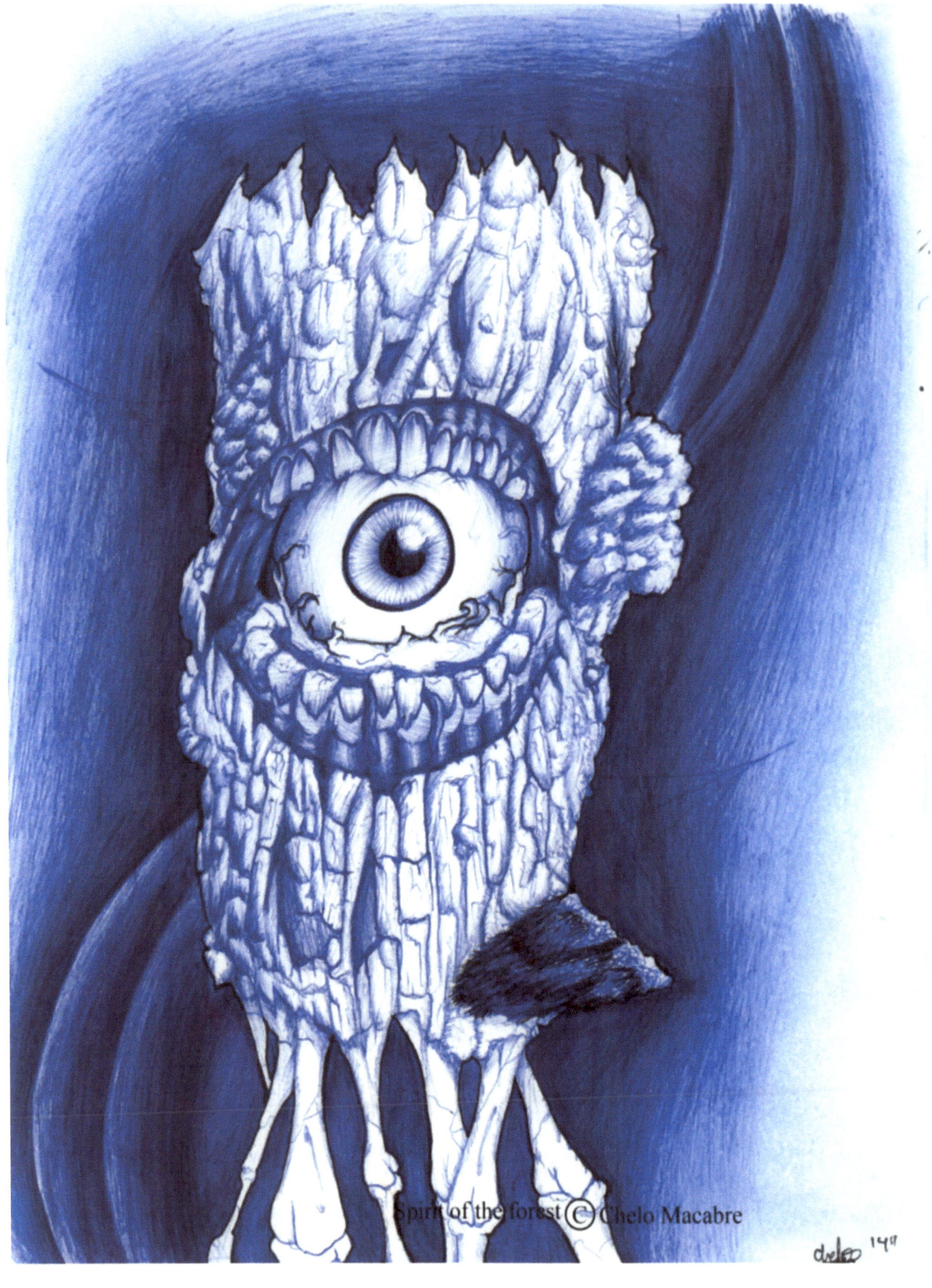

Spirit of the forest © Chelo Macabre

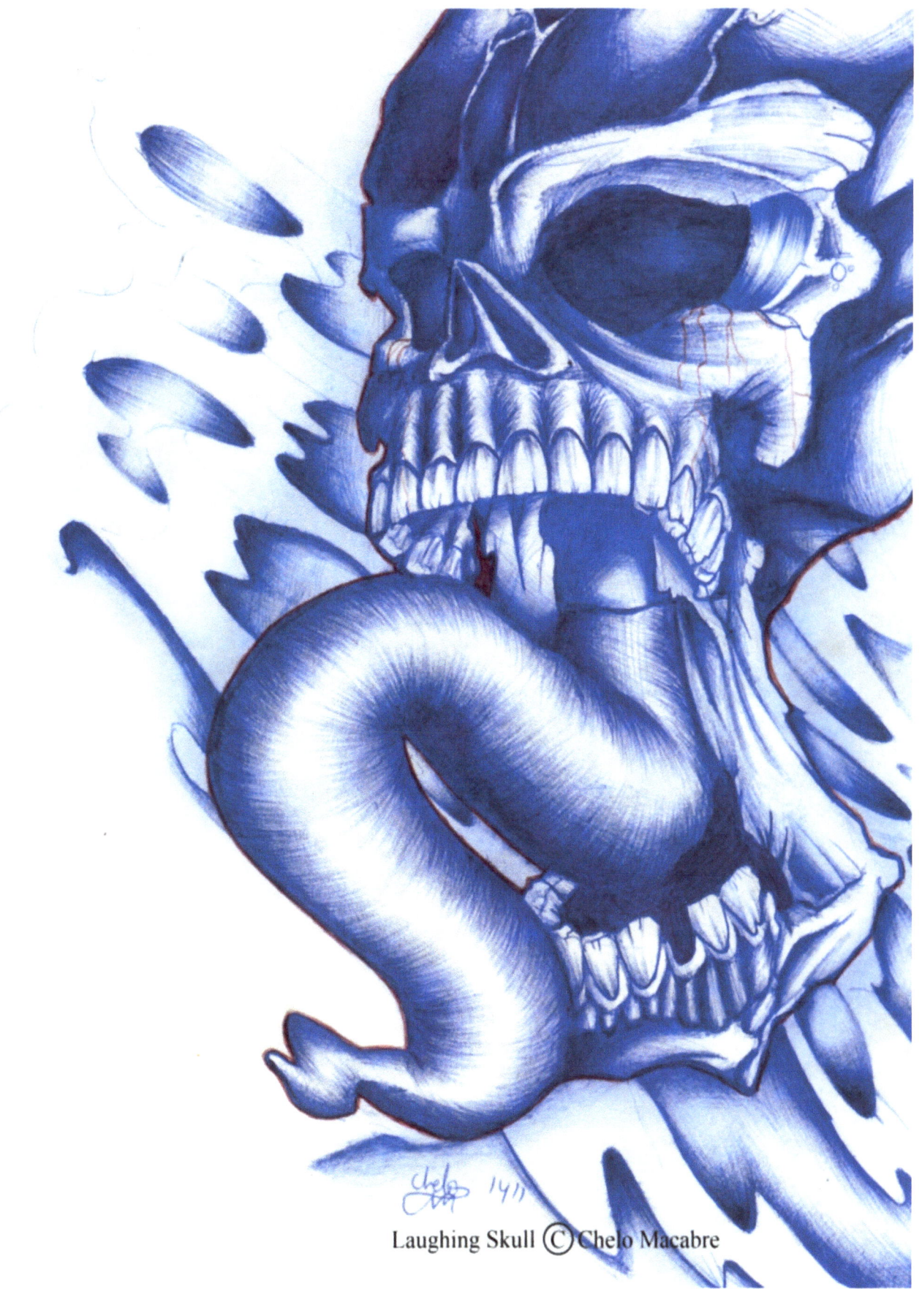

Laughing Skull © Chelo Macabre

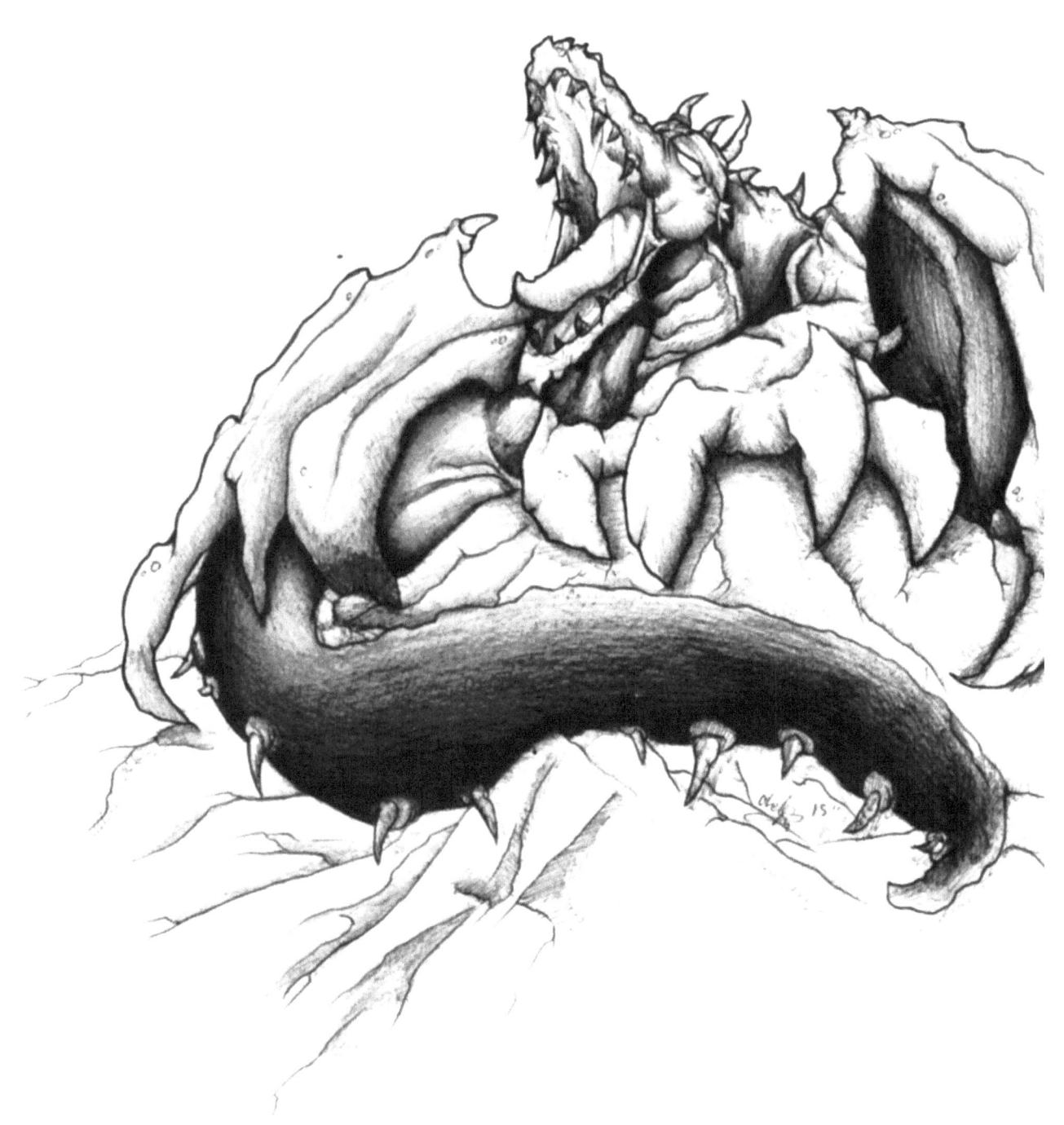

Mountain Dragon ©Chelo Macabre

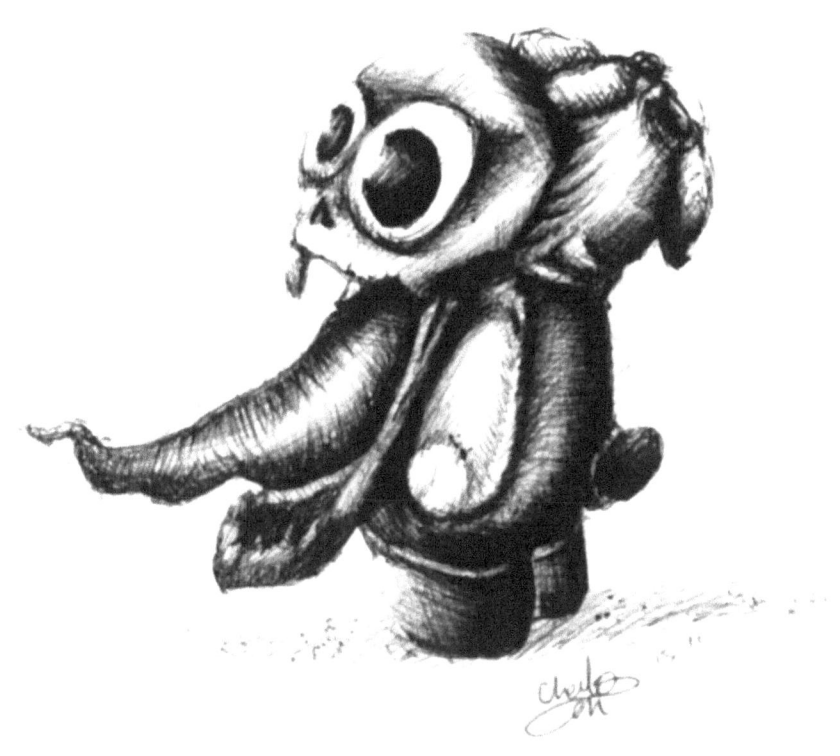

Peekaboo © Chelo Macabre

# About the Author

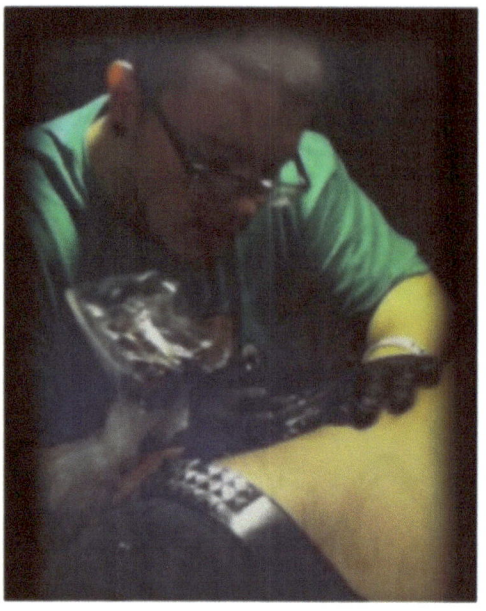

 My name is Chelo Macabre and I'm obsessed with art. I've drawn ever since I can remember and have felt a deep unconditional love for creating. My life revolves around six things, my Lord, my family, my art, music, the horror genre/ halloween, and video games (especially the Legend of Zelda series).

 I wrote this book because I really enjoy seeing other people succeed, especially other artists. I would love for this book to make at least one other artist's life just a tiny bit better. I believe that as artists we are a community and I have tons of love for every single member of it. God Bless!